Bitchcraft

SIMPLE SPELLS FOR EVERYDAY ANNOYANCES & SWEET REVENGE

KERRY COLBURN

HOUGHTON MIFFLIN HARCOURT
BOSTON   NEW YORK   2019

For information about permission to reproduce selections
from this book, write to trade.permissions@hmhco.com or to
Permissions, Houghton Mifflin Harcourt Publishing Company,
3 Park Avenue, 19th Floor, New York, New York 10016.

hmhbooks.com

Library of Congress Cataloging-in-Publication Data is available.

ISBN: 978-0-358-19698-3 (hbk); 978-0-358-19855-0 (ebk)

Book design by Rachel Marek
Book packaged by Girl Friday Productions

Printed in the United States of America
WZA 10 9 8 7 6 5 4 3 2 1

CONTENTS

THE DAILY GRIND

Bad Behavior

Unsavory Service

WORK

Disagreeable Coworkers

Bad Bosses

LOVE & LUST

Dating Disappointments

Underperforming Partners

Ugly Breakups

HOME

Trouble Inside

Trouble Outside

ON THE GO

Driving Debacles

Trouble in Transit

Vacation Blunders

INTRODUCTION

Tell me: Who among us isn't wronged on a daily basis?

Wouldn't you love to get sweet revenge on the people who drive you crazy on any given day? The ones who really deserve a little payback for their bad behavior?

I'm here to tell you: you can. We all have the power within to do just that, and it doesn't take magic. All you need is the help of a little Bitchcraft.

Women everywhere have taken back the word "bitch" and are done being accommodating. Gone is Ms. Nice Girl, who apologizes for other people's mistakes or looks the other way when someone else takes the credit that's rightfully hers. This bitch is ready to roar, unafraid to wield her power when someone intentionally crosses her.

Bitchcraft is here to inspire every woman to use *her own inner power* to get back at all the people who do her wrong in big or small ways. Whether it's an evil ex, a bad barista, a loud movie talker, or a coworker who stole your thunder, don't turn the other cheek. Screw that! Harness your innate badassery and use your Bitchcraft!

The spells in this book are simple and easy to perform to ensure you don't spend more time or energy than necessary on the suckers who screw with you. Some are quick hexes—short incantations you can recite on the go—and some are longer rituals, including a few ingredients or props to intensify the results. But there's no need to gather eye of newt or other obscure items. While you'll see suggestions for

common herbs like sage, rosemary, or thyme, as well as essential oils or candles (all of which have been used in spells and rituals for centuries), none of these is required. Your intention is the most important element in making Bitchcraft work, so if you don't have one of the items on hand, don't let it stop you. You can just say the words, or substitute a different item that speaks to you. (And of course, use care and your good common sense when using candles or lighters.)

Similarly, an altar is not necessary to perform Bitchcraft. But because you are channeling your strength and intention to right the wrongs of others, it's best to do your spells in a place where you feel powerful and in control—whether that's in your boudoir, at your workplace, or in front of your KitchenAid mixer.

Speaking of power, what's better than one strong female spell-caster? Several! Yes, you can share your Bitchcraft with other like-minded ladies for extra power. Gather your gals for a self-care coven and talk about which spell in this book each of you needs most. Then you can either recite the spells in unison or alternate taking the lead, with the rest adding power with their intentions and visualizations. Either way, the joining up of several women with the goal of setting things straight will add extra oomph to the work at hand. (And yes, it's safe to perform Bitchcraft while under the influence of a nice glass of merlot.)

It's important to note there's nothing truly harmful happening here. After all, some believe that anything you put out into the universe—positive or negative—comes back to you threefold, and even though Bitchcraft is its own modern branch of the magic tree, who wants to take that chance? Instead, the revenge offered here is of a gentler variety, designed to fit the crime at hand. Just a little tit for tat, if you will, for the twit who shouldn't have transgressed.

So get ready to cast some well-deserved spells on those who purposely cross you today! Turn off your phone, set your mind to the problem you've encountered, visualize its annoying source, and send a little psychic jab to the wrongdoer with the help of these spells and hexes. Then move on with your day, and with your life, feeling like the strong, unstoppable, superior being you are. You've got this!

Spells

There are Mondays, and then there are days that just *feel* like Mondays. Days when things seem to be conspiring against you and stubbornly refusing to go your way. You wind up stuck in traffic, get the runaround on the phone, miss the elevator, have bad service at the restaurant. It's one thing when it feels like a general "Mercury in retrograde" moment, though, and quite another when there is a very specific person to blame! If you've been brought low by someone who could've—nay, should've!—tried a smidge harder, right the wrong with a dash of revenge.

Bad Behavior

INCONSIDERATE
CELL-PHONE TALKER

Do we *all* need to know about that stranger's blood-test results, impending breakup, weekend plans, work crisis, or opinion on the latest Avengers movie? Apparently so. Certain people in modern society feel it's their God-given right to yak at full volume on their cell, even when in an enclosed space with others. While they may be acceptable in large, open places or in one's own vehicle, we all know conversations should be curtailed on the bus, train, plane, restaurant, coffee shop, waiting room, or other cozy place. Right? If you're getting a migraine from someone gabbing loudly about their latest sexcapade or what they had for lunch, turn their volume down a notch with this spell. Buh-bye.

May your cell plan be switched
(Without you knowing),
So that while you chatter,
Your bill just keeps growing.

TOXIC MALE

OK, buddy, what year is it? It's the year d-bags are held accountable for making progress as humans and ditching the inappropriate remarks, that's what year it is. It was never OK to catcall, or to make sexist comments on a woman's body, walk, outfit, abilities, or anything. But today, we're calling out that kind of caveman comportment like never before. Next time a guy tells you to smile more, talk less, look different, or give him whatever attention he so dearly craves, he'll get back more than he bargained for.

YOU'LL NEED

A nail, pin, or thumbtack
A white candle (or any candle placed atop something white)
A book, magazine, or other item featuring a strong woman
(Michelle Obama's autobiography will do nicely)
Matches or a lighter

Stick the nail into the side of the candle and place the candle atop the book or magazine. Light the wick while you visualize a shaft of bright light illuminating the offending male. Then say this spell:

It's time to evolve!
   It doesn't take a genius.
'Til then, you'll have problems
Involving your penis.

REPEATED CAR-ALARM OFFENDER

Almost no sound is more annoying than the shrill bleat of a car alarm. And, as if on purpose, they seem to go off in the middle of an important call or right as you're drifting off to sleep. Just how sensitive does a car need to be? If you've found a particular vehicle to be a repeat offender, you'd better sound the alarm in a different sense.

YOU'LL NEED

A piece of paper and a pen
The license plate number or make and model of the car
A plastic bag
A generous pinch of cayenne pepper

On the paper, write down the license plate number or make and model, then tear the paper into pieces. Put the pieces into the bag, along with the cayenne pepper, and seal. Shake the bag three times while saying this hex:

May someone accidentally scratch your car, leaving an apologetic note with a completely illegible phone number.

LOUD MOVIE TALKER

With all the streaming video these days, why don't people who are compelled to talk during movies *just stay home*? If you've splurged to see a film on the big screen, you want the whole experience: hot popcorn, a center seat, and surround sound. But the sound you don't want to be surrounded by? That yapper yakking at full volume about the drive time to the theater, their outrage at movie prices, how difficult it is to find parking in this part of town, or worse yet, plot spoilers for this very film! Time to turn down that loud talker's volume—before they spoil the ending. Glare in the offender's general direction while saying this hex under your breath:

You had this hex coming;
*   I'd simply no choice.*
When you wake up tomorrow,
You'll have lost your voice.

FRENEMY WHO CONSTANTLY CRITICIZES YOUR CHOICES

We all have that one person in our lives, don't we? The friend who we really should cut loose, but we don't. We like her, sometimes we have fun with her, and we have mutual friends in common . . . so we keep making excuses for her and keep her in our circle. But the truth is, she always has an opinion when it comes to you and your choices—and it is rarely a positive one. She has "constructive criticism" for everything from your career and your love life to whether those shoes go with your outfit. Somehow, every time you talk to her, you end up feeling just a little bit bad about yourself—and that's not cool. Give your frenemy the cold shoulder with this spell.

YOU'LL NEED
A piece of paper and a pen
Your freezer

On the paper, write down the last critical thing your frenemy said to you, something that hurt your feelings. Then bury the paper deep in your freezer, maybe behind that bag of kale and cauliflower from 2009, and say this spell:

Our friendship could be a good one,
But you've spoiled it with
dysfunction.
Next time you're somewhere fancy?
An embarrassing wardrobe malfunction.

Unsavory Service

BARISTA WHO RUINS YOUR DRINK

It's the little things in life. Treating yourself to a nice coffee on a gray morning is one of those small pleasures that can really set you off on the right foot. So when a disinterested barista does such a terrible job on your latte that it's undrinkable, then just shrugs when you tell them so, it is not the ideal start to the day. That's a little thing that deserves a little hex. Picture the caffeinated culprit and say these words:

May all taste bitter to you today, no matter how much sugar you add.

CONDESCENDING BARTENDER OR BOUNCER

There's nothing like a whiff of power to turn some people into absolute a-holes . . . especially the "nonpower power" that comes with being a bartender or bouncer at a popular hot spot. Suddenly, an average Joe thinks they're a ruler on high who is entitled to influence anyone's evening for better or worse. If you've been on the receiving end of some serious attitude (while certain young girls in minidresses get the royal treatment), it's time to knock somebody down a peg.

YOU'LL NEED

A straw or swizzle stick from the bar
A glass with any liquid inside (if you can ever get a drink!)
The first name of the offender

Using the straw, stir the drink three times counterclockwise while saying the name of the offender. Then offer the universe this spell:

> *Your attitude's atrocious,*
> *But you could've fought it.*
> *Now all your cash earnings*
> *Will soon get an audit.*

STYLIST WHO TURNS YOUR 'DO INTO A DON'T

You booked an appointment months ago, for the day of an important event. You raced here from work. You shelled out significant scratch for a stylist who was supposedly *ah*-mazing. And what did you get? Disaster! Whether the color is brassy, the cut is unflattering, or—worst of the worst—your bangs are too short, you have been seriously wronged. Unless your big plans involve a pom-pom hat (unlikely), you are stuck. The stylist, though? Snippy McSnipperpants seems positively pleased with this shoddy work! Today, your stylist is going to get something other than an undeserved 18 percent tip.

YOU'LL NEED
A strand of your own hair
The stylist's business card (or write their name on a piece of paper)
A small mirror
A red candle (or any candle placed atop something red)
Matches or a lighter

Wrap a strand of your hair around the offending stylist's card and place it on the mirror. Put the candle on top. As you light it, look down at your horrific hairstyle in the mirror and repeat this spell:

*B*ad hair for me?
Just you wait and see.
When this candle I blow,
You'll get ten bad hair days in a row!

SADISTIC PERSONAL TRAINER

OK, you know they're supposed to hurt you a little. But this is *beyond*. You signed up for personal training at the gym because you wanted to step it up a bit and see better results. For *yourself*. Instead, you ended up getting paired with a show-off hard body who seems to want mostly to prove they're stronger than you. (You already knew that, by the way.) Time to flex your hex muscles! Do your best warrior pose while saying this aloud:

May your protein powder mysteriously backfire, causing you to gain flab, not muscle. And may your favorite sport leggings have a hole in the crotch that you don't notice until the middle of class.

TELEMARKETER WHO WON'T GIVE UP

You know when you hear that telltale telemarketer pause when you pick up the phone. You should've known better than to answer an unknown number! But really, are people still trying to sell things via cold calls? And do they think you're going to change your mind if they call again, and again, and again? Of course, the situation only gets worse during election season. If you're getting repeated calls at inopportune times for things you don't want—even after you've told them not to call again—target the offending tele-annoyer with this curse.

YOU'LL NEED
Your phone
A silk scarf or cloth

Wrap your phone in the scarf, place it in a happy place in your home, like on your bed, and then say these lines:

> *You've called so many times*
> *It's become unhealthy.*
> *So you'll accidentally text your parents*
> *A way inappropriate selfie.*

CUSTOMER-SERVICE REP WHO GIVES YOU THE RUNAROUND

These days, when so much can be handled online, you really have to steel yourself to place an actual call to a customer-service line. Whether it's to cancel a plane flight, change your phone plan, or deal with a defective product, you know it won't be easy. But sometimes it's worse than that. You sit on hold listening to something terrible (is that a Muzak version of Pearl Jam?), being told every thirty seconds that your call is important, and meanwhile life is passing you by. If, after all that, you get a clueless customer-service rep who doesn't understand, won't help, or puts you back on hold to talk to an elusive "supervisor"? Strike back with a fitting spell.

YOU'LL NEED
Your phone
A black candle (or any candle placed atop something black)
Matches or a lighter

Resist the urge to throw your phone across the room. Instead place it next to the candle. Light the candle, take a few deep, soothing breaths while envisioning what the offending rep might look like, and say:

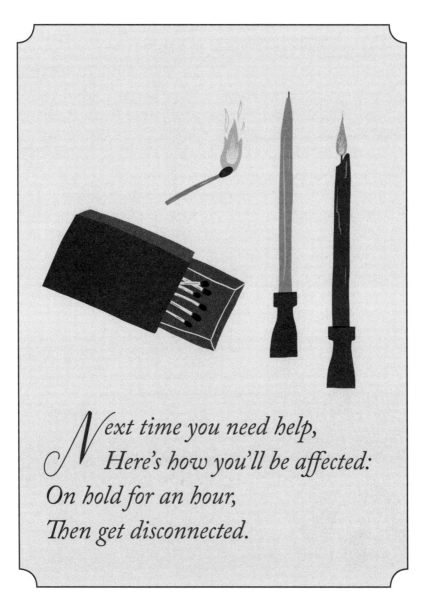

*N*ext time you need help,
   Here's how you'll be affected:
On hold for an hour,
Then get disconnected.

SWINDLING MECHANIC

You thought we were beyond this era. How does the stereotype of the dishonest, misogynist mechanic still prove true? If you've left your beloved wheels in the care of someone who has returned to you a misdiagnosis, inflated bill, or an expensive and unnecessary recommendation for what to do next, with a side of condescension, throw a (metaphorical) wrench right back at them.

YOU'LL NEED
Your car keys
The bill from the repair shop

Wrap the keys in the bill and grip the bundle tightly in your fist while visualizing the mechanic. Then say this spell:

When you go through the car wash
Before hitting the town,
You'll realize too late
Your back window was down.

SNOBBY HOST OR HOSTESS AT HOT RESTAURANT OR CLUB

Sure, they're young and beautiful. And their job grants them an inordinate amount of clout for someone so inexperienced in the ways of the world. But really? Don't they know you can't always judge a person by her sensible flats? You try to get a table for two, and they not only look you up and down, you swear they downright scoff. You may not be an A-lister, but you *are* a paying customer, and there's no need to be so catty. If you've gotten the brush-off from a hostess who's gotten too big for her Jimmy Choos, or a host who needs to polish both his Warby Parkers and his manners, remind them that karma—like someone else we know—is a bitch. Picture their face and say this hex:

The next time you go on a date, you'll be seated at the worst possible table, so close to the bathrooms that you can hear people pee.

PAINFULLY SLOW
CHECKOUT CLERK

There's slow, and there's painfully slow, and then there's painfully slow *on purpose*. You know the type: smacking gum, scrolling through Instagram, barely acknowledging your presence. And doing their job as slowly as humanly possible, as if taking you down into their own misery will somehow make their shift more bearable. Aren't you the customer, and in return for spending money in this establishment, shouldn't you be treated with courteous efficiency by someone who appreciates that you have a life to get on with? If you've been the victim of the slowest checkout ever, speed home to perform this spell.

YOU'LL NEED
Tape
Your receipt from the store
An 8½ × 11 piece of paper

Tape the receipt to the larger piece of paper, then fold it paper-airplane style. Go to a far corner of the room and send it flying, picturing the offending clerk in your mind. When it crashes, say this spell:

You didn't work quickly
Or respect my time,
So your day off will involve
An epic Target line.

UNHELPFUL
HEALTH-CARE PROVIDER

It's already a pain to have to go to the doctor or the dentist. After scrambling for an appointment, you end up in a waiting room, leafing through ancient *People* magazines and wondering why they couldn't just text you that the doctor was running forty-five minutes late. But when you finally get to see your provider and they rush you through, leaving you feeling as if you didn't get the care you deserved—much less the time to ask any questions? Not acceptable. Give them a taste of their own medicine with this simple but powerful hex:

For every patient you rush
through today
Without the proper care,
May you get a day of itchy symptoms
In that place we call "down there."

Essential Empowerment Spell

If your daily routine is still bringing you down, use this spell to rise above. You'll sail through annoyances so that you're ready to take on the important work (and fun) of the day.

_____

YOU'LL NEED

A piece of paper and a pen
A personal item that reminds you of your daily routine
(such as your favorite mug or your handbag)
Matches or a lighter
A white candle (or any candle placed atop something white)

_____

On the paper, write down a quick description of your perfect day. Roll up the paper and place it inside the personal item. Light the candle and picture yourself at a point in that ideal day, bathed in light. Take three deep breaths, then say this spell:

Spirits, protect me from the daily minutiae
that can make a bright mood and good intentions
fade into dark. Remind me that at any time of
the day, I have the power to turn my own light up
brighter and illuminate my path.

Spells

There's a reason they call it *work*. It isn't all fun and games. Sure, you expect to do your duties, stay late when needed, and pull your weight at your job in return for a reasonable paycheck. You know there will be bad days (and bad meetings!) as well as good, and you're OK with that. But evil managers, unhelpful assistants, ridiculous clients, insufferable suck-ups, or colleagues who try to steal your thunder shouldn't be part of the package. If you're saddled with any of these characters at work, it can make a long, hard day even worse. Use these spells to show your coworkers that you mean business.

Disagreeable Coworkers

UBER-COMPETITIVE COLLEAGUE WHO UNDERMINES YOU

Oh, the office suck-up. Do they think you don't see what they're up to? This crafty colleague tries to take credit for every bit of work in the office, especially when a supervisor is present. You can make a great point, offer a solution, or explain a new idea—and within five minutes, they reiterate it and try to pass it off as their own. You are sick and tired of them trying to steal the spotlight without actually earning it. It's time for them to make a misstep. Focus your energy and anger in their direction while saying this hex:

The next time you take credit for my idea, you will experience an epic autocorrect fail and send something really offensive to our boss.

i look forward to sleeping with you

*SPEAKING not sleeping!!

COWORKER WHO KEEPS EMAILING WHILE YOU'RE ON VACATION

We all know that person who can't stop talking about how hard they work. The one who answers messages at midnight, makes sure they send large group emails on the weekend, and brags about their dedication to the job. It's all good if they want a skewed work-life balance. Maybe that's even your style, now and then. But when you're on vacation? That's sacred. You wait all year for a fantastic getaway; the last thing you need is someone spoiling it, especially with nonessential messages. When someone compromises your time off with things that could wait, teach them a lesson in restraint.

YOU'LL NEED

A piece of paper and a pen
Your coworker's name and email address
A glass of cold water
A pinch of salt

On the paper, write the offender's info, then drop it into the glass of water and sprinkle it with the salt. As you watch it get soaked, offer up this spell:

*T*ake a chill pill! This ain't brain
    surgery.
We can all use a day off (especially me).
Because you have bugged me
And ruined my stay,
On your next vacation,
It will rain every day.

IT PERSON WHO RUINED YOUR PRESENTATION

Every time you call with a computer problem, their only response is to turn your machine off and on again. (OK, it usually works, but *still*.) They are not known for being super helpful. But this was your chance to shine: a big presentation with fancy animated PowerPoint slides and everything. All they had to do was make sure the technical stuff worked properly. Whether it was a bungled projector, faulty speaker, or connection snafu, their incompetence put a serious damper on your moment in the spotlight.

YOU'LL NEED
A small technical item (mouse, cable, thumb drive)
A piece of dark cloth

Wrap the technical item in the cloth and put it in a drawer where it can stay for at least twenty-four hours (ideally far from your own desk). Then say this spell:

I was supposed to shine brightly,
But you made me red-faced.
Tonight you'll go home
To find Netflix erased.

WORK-PARTY EMBARRASSMENT

We're all grown-ups here, yes? That means we should be able to behave with some level of decorum at a work shindig, no matter how much free booze is flowing. But there's always one partygoer who goes a little too far: making inappropriate jokes, spilling their drinks, complaining loudly about coworkers, and generally behaving badly. This time, that person was all over you—sloshing a drink on your outfit and ruining your good time. Better get them into a cab and out of your evening. As you send them on their way, whisper this hex:

Tomorrow morning, may you be out of both coffee and ibuprofen, and may you spill your hangover cure all over your keyboard.

TEAM MEMBER WHO DOESN'T PULL THEIR WEIGHT

Just like the old days of the school science fair: on a group project, there is always, *always* someone who drags down the whole team. They either talk too much (but don't *say* anything), shoot down other people's ideas (but don't offer their own), don't do their share of the work, or are just absent when you need them to be present. If they're truly inept, and not just a slacker, they can even make the project worse. If you are spending valuable time and energy making up for someone who contributes next to nothing, it's their turn to feel the consequences.

YOU'LL NEED

A printout of one of the offender's emails
(the more annoying the better)
A cup of vinegar
A timer or timer app

Read a couple of lines from the email aloud. Then tear it up and put it in the cup of vinegar. Place the cup near a timer for one minute, and say this spell:

Your work is a downer,
And your attitude's not great.
When you need to leave early,
You'll have to stay late.

SLOPPY ASSISTANT

It's so exciting to have an assistant! Except when they're awful. In that case, sometimes the help you get is negated by the messes you have to clean up. Does your assistant lose phone messages, cancel your print jobs, miss deadlines, or say the absolutely wrong thing in meetings? Do you find that when they are out, your day actually runs more smoothly? If you've reached the breaking point with a bungling assistant who just doesn't cut it, try this spell . . . and then start looking at résumés.

I've given you chances,
At least twenty, or more.
It's clearly time
To show you the door.
But since you are here
Messing things up for me,
May you get a job transfer
To Schenectady.

TIRESOME WORKPLACE GOSSIP

Everyone loves a bit of harmless gossip now and again, especially about a coworker. But there is a time, a place, and a limit. If someone at your workplace is constantly telling tall tales, spreading dirty rumors, or taking you aside to tell you things you'd really rather not know, it's time to shut them down. After all, if someone talks trash about all those other people, do you really think they're not doing the same about you? Get this meddlesome mudslinger to stop stirring the pot before you end up burned (if you haven't been already).

YOU'LL NEED
A pot
Water
A wooden spoon

Fill the pot with water (no heating necessary) and stir in a clockwise direction, channeling the witches from *Macbeth*.

Double double, toil and trouble,
Fire burn and cauldron bubble,
To put your thoughtless talk to an end,
An embarrassing company-wide
email you'll send!

OBNOXIOUS OFFICE MATE

Oh. Em. Gee. It's bad enough that you have to share close quarters (what you would give for a real door!)—but with this clown? Whether it's a shared office, adjoining cubicles, or adjacent desks in a fishbowl, there is nothing worse than having to comingle—closely comingle—with a particularly unsavory colleague. Name your annoying trait: there's the nose picker, the loud talker, the stinky gym-goer, the whistler, the open-mouthed chewer, the gum smacker. If you've had to listen to embarrassing personal phone calls at full volume or smell exactly what they're having for lunch (tuna *again*?), you know it's time for a strong separation spell.

YOU'LL NEED

A few drops of rosemary oil (or a pinch of dried rosemary)
A ball of yarn or string

Sprinkle the rosemary oil on the yarn. After work hours, tie one end of the yarn to your office mate's chair. Then wrap it around their desk, lamp, computer, phone, etc. Next, stand at your own desk, take a deep breath, and offer the hex on the next page to the universe (or at least the office). When you're done, remove the yarn and dispose of it somewhere far away from your work space.

May your computer act wonky
 And same with your phone
Until the only solution
Is to just work from home.

INAPPROPRIATE
WORKPLACE FLIRTER

There's a fine line between friendly and flirting, isn't there? We all know when it's been crossed, though—especially at work, where people really should know better. If someone at your workplace has been a little *too* friendly, it's important to set them straight, fast. When talk doesn't do the trick, try a spell to put that overly personal person in their place.

YOU'LL NEED
A piece of paper and a pen
A glass of water
Three peppercorns
Alka-Seltzer or other tummy tablets

On the paper, write down the last inappropriate thing this person said to you. Then place the paper facedown, with the glass of water on top of it. Drop the peppercorns into the glass, followed by the Alka-Seltzer. Then say this spell:

You like to make comments
About how I dress,
But the next time it happens
You'll get IBS.

PUSHY MANSPLAINER

You can hold your own. You're smart, confident, and not afraid to speak your mind. You also realize that you don't know everything, so you're happy to learn from others who have more knowledge or experience. But come on! There's always that one guy in the office who firmly believes he's an expert on everything—when he's not. He derails meetings and pulls focus with his long-winded explanations of how something works, when you know *exactly* how that thing works. No amount of pushback seems to stop this pushy gasbag, so give him a little message that requires no explanation. Visualize him talking (always talking!) while saying this hex:

The next time you start explaining something obvious, you'll get a sudden, epic, and noisy bout of flatulence that you cannot control.

Bad Bosses

BOSS WHO DENIED YOUR PROMOTION/RAISE

You're valuable. Of course you are! And you were pretty sure your boss knew this, too. So, naturally, after all you've done, you were expecting a nice reward at review time: a bump in pay, a new title, or both. But at the long-anticipated meeting, your boss pulled a fast one and you left empty-handed. Give them a taste of how they've made you feel with this spell.

YOU'LL NEED

A pair of gloves
Your boss's business card (or write their name on a slip of paper)
Your business card (or write your name and title on a slip of paper)
A stack of cash (any denominations or currencies will do)
Ribbon

Put the gloves side by side, palms up, with your boss's business card on one and yours on the other. Place a stack of cash on top of your boss's card. Wait ten seconds, then move it to your own card. Remove your boss's card and bind the two gloves together with the ribbon, keeping your card and the cash sandwiched in between. Then say this spell:

I'm left empty-handed;
  It was so lame and unkind.
When you next go to buy something,
Your card will be declined.

  My prospects soon will rise
    And your star will fall.
  When you need that next job,
  Don't give me a call.

INTERVIEWER WHO STRUNG YOU ALONG

You nailed that interview! You had all the right qualifications, prepared perfectly, and wore your best power outfit. Your answers were thoughtful, witty, maybe even genius. You connected with the interviewer, and they maybe even hinted that the job was yours. But after they strung you along through two more rounds? You got a courtesy email—and not the job.

YOU'LL NEED
Your interviewer's initials
A white candle (or any candle placed atop something white)
A butter knife or toothpick
A piece of string
Matches or a lighter

Carve your interviewer's initials into the candle with the knife. Wrap the string around the candle while channeling all your frustration. Light the candle and say this spell:

You strung me along,
So your day will soon worsen.
May you be stuck in the elevator
With your least favorite person.

MEETING-HAPPY SUPERVISOR

Can we all agree that, most of the time, meetings are unnecessary? So much could be handled via email. And yet, hour after hour, we sit in confabs and conferences both IRL and virtual. We even have meetings about having too many meetings! And often, the real work has to wait until after six p.m., when you are finally meeting free. Alas, part of the problem is that some people—like this particular supervisor, for example—seem to like meetings. Meetings give them a sense of purpose. Often these are people who like to feel in charge and *really* like hearing themselves talk. How to get them to see the light? Much like training a puppy, you need them to receive a gentle but consistent punishment every time they exhibit the undesired behavior. Let's teach some cause and effect with this hex:

Each dumb meeting will cause a zit.
After five o'clock? You'll get two.
Let's hope it doesn't take many more
For you to get a damn clue.

PASSIVE-AGGRESSIVE MANAGER

Maybe you thought an aggressive manager was the worst kind. But then you encountered a *passive*-aggressive one. The worst thing about this personality type is that you're never quite sure where you stand, so you end up feeling awkward and unbalanced. Was that a compliment, or an insult? Did they like the work you did, or was it terrible? Are they grooming you for a promotion, or trying to find a way to fire you? Who knows? If you've reached your limit with a supervisor who plays endless mind games, get clarity with this spell.

YOU'LL NEED

A deck of cards
A bay leaf
Your manager's business card (or simply their name written on a piece of paper)

Place the deck of cards on a table and cut them. Put the bay leaf and business card on top of one stack, then close the deck. Put the deck on a windowsill and say this incantation, then leave it there through your next workday.

If the weather was sunny,
*   You'd tell me it's raining.*
Your mind games with me
Are physically draining.
But you'll soon be out of office,
There's no use complaining:
You'll be forced to attend
Dreaded management training.

PERSON WHO SCREWED
WITH YOUR HOURS

Not everyone has a nine-to-five job. If someone else is in charge of your shifts, hours, weekend work, and overtime, you rely on them to be considerate and reasonable—or, at the very least, sane. But looking at your upcoming schedule? You've been screwed. Totally screwed! Whether you don't have enough hours to pay the bills, or you've been scheduled so heavily that you'll have no life for the foreseeable future, it's unfair. If you can't get things back on track, at least for the time being, get some payback with this spell.

YOU'LL NEED

A screw

A glass jar

Vinegar

A calendar (the old-fashioned paper kind—you can print out this month from the internet if you need to)

Drop the screw into the jar and add enough vinegar to cover it. Place the jar on top of the calendar, turned to the week or month affected by the sadistic schedule-maker. Then say the spell on the next page. Keep the jar as is until your schedule changes.

You like to screw with a schedule?
This spell does that to you—
As your most important engagements
Disappear mysteriously from view.

OVERLY DEMANDING CLIENT

The customer isn't always right. But when you work with demanding customers or clients, you know that part of the job is making sure they're happy, even when they're wrong. However, things can go too far. If you have to deal with someone who is overly demanding, rude, unreasonable, condescending, or just downright mean, you can't always turn the other cheek. If you must play nice at work, at least give them a little taste of naughty with this spell.

YOU'LL NEED

A piece of paper and a pen
One drop of lavender essential oil (or a pinch of dried lavender)

Think about the bad behavior and how it made you feel. Then, on the paper, write the word "STOP" in capital letters. Fold it as many times as you can, folding away from you. When the paper is as small as you can make it, add 1 drop of the essential oil, and then dispose of the paper while saying this spell:

You treat me poorly
No matter what I do.
After your next tirade,
You'll step in dog poo.

Essential Empowerment Spell

If you still need more help in the work arena, don't fret—here's a spell that's more useful than the most faithful assistant and more beneficial than a mental-health day.

YOU'LL NEED

A piece of paper and a pen
An item from your current workplace
Matches or a lighter
A green candle (or any candle placed atop something green)

On the paper, write down your absolute dream job, then put it faceup on top of the item from your current job. Light the candle and picture yourself in a bright-green spotlight, working at your dream job. Take three deep breaths, then say this spell aloud:

Spirits, protect me from awful colleagues, bad bosses, glass ceilings, and dead-end jobs. May I remember that I can do anything I set my mind to, and help me rise to my full potential in any work path I choose.

Spells

Rarely do we desire revenge more than with matters of the heart—or at least the body. Whether it's a run-in with an evil ex, a truly disappointing hookup, or a date who is clearly not their profile picture, there are always irksome bumps on the road to love. Make the journey smoother by knocking a few underserving characters out of the way with these spells. Remember, you hold the power, and only the worthy should hold your heart (or your other amazing parts)!

Dating Disappointments

DATE WHO "FORGETS" TO PAY

After insisting on a spendy restaurant, then ordering an over-priced entree plus three twenty-dollar cocktails and a dessert (which they didn't share), your date claims they forgot their wallet—leaving you stuck with the bill. If this sounds familiar, you've got yourself a freeloader, and you've got to free yourself.

YOU'LL NEED
The receipt from your last date
A penny
A fireproof pan or dish (the sink will also do nicely)
Matches or a lighter

Put the receipt atop the penny in the pan. Set the receipt aflame while saying this spell:

> *As burned by you,*
> *Now you by me;*
> *Your debt will increase*
> *As I walk away free!*

DISAPPOINTING
HOOKUP

Oh, awful sex. We've all been there, and it's sooo awkward. Sometimes the problem is mutual—chemistry is off, too much tequila was consumed, a roommate walks in unexpectedly, that sort of thing. But other times—let's admit it—it's not you! Did you fall victim to someone who had no game, no technique, and worst of all, no consideration for your needs? No excuses! Let them know the score, so that their next encounter misses.

YOU'LL NEED

Your best lingerie or other sexy attire
A piece of paper and a pen

Put on your sexy stuff. On the paper, write the culprit's name. Then flip the paper over and write a favorite sex act on the back. Fold up the paper and tear it into tiny pieces while saying this spell:

*Into my bedsheets you will not get;
I'm saving myself for a better duet.
But next time you get a chance to score,
She will come first, then roll over
and snore.*

HOTTIE WHO DISSES YOUR LOOK

"Oh, is that what you're wearing?" It's bad enough when you hear that from a friend, but from a cutie you're interested in? The worst. A flip comment about a hairstyle, makeup, an outfit, or (gasp) weight—especially when you think you're looking particularly fierce—can shake a girl's confidence. But not yours. Use this spell to keep it strong.

YOU'LL NEED
A hand mirror
Your own fabulousness

First, find some flattering lighting and take a good long look at yourself in the mirror, noting all your wonderful physical attributes, ideally out loud. Be specific! Call out your luminous skin, your sparkling eyes, your kissable pout, your adorable freckles. Then turn the mirror outward and recite this simple incantation, knowing a better person is on the horizon.

Those worthy of my attention
Will soon make themselves known.
Disrespect me and spend
The next fifty nights alone.

DATING-APP DECEIVER

When your date walked into the restaurant, you didn't recognize them—even though you've carefully studied that profile picture. Who *is* this person? Did they use a picture of a friend, Photoshop, or a snap from the pre-digital era? You're not superficial. The problem is, if they fib about what they look like at the outset, what might they lie about later? Suddenly, it turns out your "entrepreneur" is actually "living in their parents' basement" and that love of travel extends only to an addiction to *House Hunters International*. This person is a deceiver and an utter time waster. Stop them before they strike again!

YOU'LL NEED
Your phone
One sprig of sage (or a pinch of dried sage)

After returning home, pull up your deceitful date's profile on your phone. Place your phone atop the sage while saying this spell to ensure no one else gets caught in their web:

You fooled me once,
It won't happen twice.
All your dates will swipe left
Until you start playing nice.

DATE WHO BORED YOU OR CREEPED YOU OUT

Not every date can be a winner. But shouldn't they at least try? It's an unspoken but fundamental rule we all agree to: go on a date, put in an effort to be charming. It's simply unfair to find yourself with someone who makes no attempt to entertain you, offering only long-winded stories of a boring job or people you don't know. Possibly worse? The creepy date who makes weirdly sexual comments, sidles up next to you after five minutes of conversation, shows you workout photos on their phone, or just puts you on edge with skeezy behavior. If you made the effort to give yourself a killer blowout, put on a cute outfit, and leave the couch, you deserve much better than this. Turn the tables with this spell.

YOU'LL NEED

A pinch of dried thyme
Any item from the date (such as a napkin,
receipt, mint, or matches)

Sprinkle the thyme atop the other item and place it on a windowsill. Visualize your date's face and then say this spell:

That date was just awful;
    I should've stayed home.
In a cab you'll forget
Your beloved iPhone.

PERSISTENT WANNABE DATE WHO WON'T TAKE A HINT

It's nice to be wanted. But what's not nice? Having to say no, over and over, to someone who just can't—or won't—hear it. Maybe it's someone who is desperate to move past the friend zone. Maybe it's someone you went out with once and can't accept that you're just not that into them. If a pushy person is hanging around, texting too often, and generally cramping your style, release them from your spell with this one.

YOU'LL NEED
A black ribbon or string
A magnet (anything magnetic will do)
A pair of scissors

Tie the ribbon into a knot around the magnet, visualizing the unwanted suitor caught in your web of magnetism. (I mean, who can blame them?) Then, imagine them somewhere very, very far away—say, Iceland—while you say the spell below. When you're done, cut the ribbon.

We're not going to happen! Really, this is no lie.
Until your affections aim elsewhere,
you'll suffer pink eye.

PARTICULARLY BAD KISSER

You've generously given this person tons of lip service, but it's like you're in junior high all over again, playing seven minutes in heaven with a kid who seems to have no control over their own mouth. You've even offered gentle instruction, whispering helpful tips like, "Less tongue, maybe?" But there's no change. Give this saliva-soaked situation the kiss-off.

YOU'LL NEED
A stack of magazines
Your favorite lipstick or gloss
A breath mint

Flip through the magazines, tear out some pictures of appealing kiss partners, and lay your favorite three on a table. Then paint your pout with the lipstick and give each picture a big, wet smack before saying the spell below. When you're done, keep the lipstick on, pop a breath mint, and head out to find your new smooching partner.

I deserve a transporting kiss.
I can do much better than this!
By the time this week is through,
I'll be planting my lips somewhere new.

DATE WHO STOOD YOU UP

The preamble went so well: witty texts, a little flirting, a fun plan made for a night out. You wore something cute. You got there on time. You were super excited about this date! And then . . . crickets. You were left sitting alone, with no call, no text, no last-minute apologies. During the agonizing hour you waited, constantly checking your phone, other diners and waitstaff were surely feeling sorry for you. Screw that! You don't want pity. You want—nay, *need*—revenge.

YOU'LL NEED

A piece of paper and a pencil
An eraser
Three drops of eucalyptus essential oil

On the paper, write the no-show's name three times on three separate lines. Erase the name, one line at a time. After each name disappears, put one drop of the essential oil on the empty space, and repeat this spell:

You brought me pain,
So your name I erase.
Now you'll get a bad rash
In a very private place.

BACKHANDED COMPLIMENTER

Everyone likes a nice bit of admiration, but this person's praise always sounds a teeny bit like an insult. All you want to hear is something straightforwardly positive, along the lines of, "You look amazing!" Instead, you get sidewinders that are open to interpretation, like, "It's great how OK you are with dressing for comfort." Say what?

YOU'LL NEED

Five slips of paper and a pen
An envelope or sealable bag
A sprinkle of cinnamon
Something belonging to the perpetrator

On each slip of paper, write down one compliment you'd be happy to receive. Put the papers into the envelope, add the cinnamon, and seal. Then say the spell below. When you're done, leave the envelope overnight near something belonging to the perpetrator.

Sweeter things must now be said;
Real affection you must show.
I'll hear true compliments by morning
Or your nose and ear hair will overgrow.

Underperforming Partners

PARTNER WHO FORGETS
A SPECIAL OCCASION

Some couples celebrate all sorts of milestones—first meeting, first kiss, even their first "sexaversary." If a partner forgets a fun but nonessential occasion, they can probably be forgiven. Even Valentine's Day is considered less than important by some. But the big ones—your birthday and your actual anniversary—must be respected. If your partner completely forgot, or showed up with an obviously last-minute gift (like wilting carnations wrapped in plastic from the corner market), reset expectations. Especially if you went all out for them!

YOU'LL NEED
A piece of paper and a pen
Matches or a lighter
A red candle (or any candle placed atop something red)
The best gift or card you've ever received

On the paper, write the important date boldly. Light the candle and place it next to the beloved gift, focusing on how it felt to receive it. Draw a circle around the date as you say:

The day was too special
To be totally missed.
You'll fix this problem
If you want to be kissed.

Make it up to me quickly
With the right attitude,
Or you'll never see me
Again in the nude.

PARTNER WHO YOU SUSPECT MAY BE CHEATING

You've started to see signs. Perhaps there's no real proof yet, but there's some seriously suspicious activity: quickly deleted texts, unanswered phone calls late at night, evasive replies to your questions. Maybe they've also altered their look, with a fresh haircut, better outfits, a heightened exercise routine. Meanwhile, they've been strangely distant—especially in the bedroom. Could they be cheating? Don't get mad, get even.

YOU'LL NEED
A hot pepper (jalapeño, habanero, etc.)
Your partner's underpants

Wrap up the hot pepper in the underpants and say this hex:

If you're considering cheating, may you feel an acute burning sensation every time you think of going through with it.

If you're actually cheating, may that burning sensation stay with you long-term, even after a round of antibiotics.

PARTNER WHO TAKES YOU FOR GRANTED

You give, and you give, and you give some more. Meanwhile, your partner has been slacking. Perhaps you need to see more effort or enthusiasm when it comes to household duties, romance, or general relationship maintenance. Perhaps you're just feeling taken for granted, without enough thank-yous, compliments, back rubs, or date nights. Lack of appreciation is a slippery slope. If you let it go on too long, it becomes the norm—and it can be hard to get back to the way things were. Your partner ought to know how good they have it!

YOU'LL NEED
Your partner's keys
Your partner's shoes

Place the keys and shoes by the front door, facing out. Say this spell aloud. (Feel free to replace "cook dinner" with another task or perk that would please you most.)

> *You should show me more effort.*
> *You know that I'm right.*
> *You'll be compelled to cook dinner*
> *For the next seven nights.*

PARTNER'S DISAPPROVING PARENTS

Oh sure, your partner's parents are civil. But just barely. You try your best to be the ideal girlfriend and say the right things, but to no avail. Every time you get together, you field backhanded compliments about your work, your appearance, your background. Meanwhile, your love seems absolutely oblivious! If you've been saddled with disapproving partner parents, and your charming self can't seem to change their minds, stop sucking up and bring in some backup.

YOU'LL NEED

A piece of paper and a pen
Matches or a lighter
A red candle (or any candle placed atop something red)

On the paper, write a short list of your best qualities. Meditate on these and then light the candle. As it burns, picture the condescending parents in your mind and send them this hex:

Next time you're trying to impress someone, the place you go will have completely lost your reservation—and they'll be very rude about it.

COMMITMENT-PHOBIC PARTNER

It's not that all you want is for your partner to put a ring on it. (Not entirely, anyway.) You just want to know where you stand. You want a commitment of some sort! You want plans! You want to be able to talk about next month, or next year, or the distant future, without your S.O. looking like a deer in the headlights. If you've been together for a while, you shouldn't have to pussyfoot around the topic of long-term monogamy. You're a great catch. Time's ticking to lock this down.

YOU'LL NEED
A strand of your partner's hair
A ring (of any kind)
A handful of rose petals

Tie the strand of hair around the ring. Cover it with the rose petals. Close your eyes and think of the commitment you're looking for, big or small. Then offer up this spell:

> *Make up your mind,*
> *and tell me soon.*
> *Or you'll be sleeping alone*
> *By the next full moon.*

PARTNER WHO STEALS YOUR SPOTLIGHT

Everyone deserves to be put on a pedestal now and then—to be celebrated, praised, even bragged about to friends. But wait a second. When is it *your* turn? Have you been coddling and complimenting your mate to no end, making sure their talents and contributions are known far and wide, with no shout-outs in return? Do you find you're always doing what they want to do, so they can show off what they're good at? Face fact: some people are more takers and some are more givers. It's time for your partner to see the light . . . *your* light.

YOU'LL NEED
A piece of paper and a pen
A photo of you and your partner
Red ribbon
Flashlight

On the paper, take a moment to write down three wonderful and specific things about yourself: accomplishments, qualities, talents. Put the paper atop the photo and tie it with the ribbon. Then shine the flashlight on the photo while saying this spell:

*Starting tonight, you'll feel my power
And give me sincere compliments
on the hour.
You'll sing my praises like I've never seen
Until you make me feel like a queen.*

Ugly Breakups

CHEATING EX'S NEW FLAME

First, your ex cheated. The lowlife. And you're pretty sure it was with *her*. So how does it feel to bump into her—or *them!*—when you least expect it? It's the absolute worst. Of course you did your best to smile, act disinterested, and not poke their eyes out. That means you deserve to treat yourself to something nice later. But them? Give them what *they* deserve.

YOU'LL NEED

A memento of your cheating ex (such as a matchbook, photo, or ticket stub; if you've purged everything already, just draw an unflattering portrait instead)
A magazine ad (or online printout) for either erectile dysfunction or yeast infection medication

---

Put the memento on a table. Place the ad directly on top of the memento and say this curse:

Because of bad karma,
New love will be no vacation.
May your sex life be lacking
Without some serious medication.

EVIL EX

In everyone's past-relationship closet lurks a particularly awful ex, the one who treated you most unforgivably. If they wronged you big-time, it doesn't matter if it happened last week or last year—it's still painful. Bumping into this ex can fill you with feelings of ill will, especially if they had the nerve to catch you when you're feeling less than your best. But don't get mad—they don't deserve any more of your energy. Get even.

YOU'LL NEED

Scissors
An old photo of you and your ex
A piece of paper and a pen

With the scissors, cut your ex out of the photo. On the paper, write your ex's phone number backward. Fold both the cut-out photo and the paper in half, then in half again, and throw them away far from your bedroom (or ideally, far from your house) while saying this spell:

> *I'm better off without you.*
> *There is so much that you lack.*
> *Next time you fall for someone,*
> *May they never text you back.*

LOVE INTEREST
WHO GHOSTED YOU

It was entirely mutual from the get-go. There was flirting, banter, chemistry. Next there were a few naughty texts, a couple of *very* hot dates, and a delicious sleepover. Then? Radio silence. Not only are they suddenly not calling, they're not answering. For a while you made excuses, but it's become clear: this is a total freeze-out. You're left with no information, save for trolling Instagram to see if there's a new companion in posts from the weekend. You're better than that. Get your revenge on this coldhearted snake so you can move on to someone who deserves you.

YOU'LL NEED

A piece of paper and a pen
Your freezer

On the paper, write the offender's name and number, then fold it three times facing away from you. Put it in the freezer. When the paper feels as cold as their heart, take it out, hold it in your hand, say the spell, and then throw away the paper.

*D*idn't your mother teach you better
    Than to treat women this way?
I deserve nicer behavior
After our roll in the hay.
You don't seem to get it,
So this hex is my balm.
Every time you're having sex—
You'll get a call from your mom.

FORMER LOVE WHO INVITES YOU TO THEIR WEDDING

Sure, there are exes who stay civil. Maybe some exes even remain friends. But this ex? They *know* you're not friends. Which makes you wonder if that fancy envelope that arrived in the mail was truly a wedding invitation or just an expensive, calligraphy-laden opportunity to gloat. You didn't even get a plus-one! Do they imagine you can't find a date, or do they just want to see you looking forlorn at the loser table in the back? Either way, it's just tacky. They may be the one walking down the aisle, but you'll always be the one with more style.

YOU'LL NEED
Red pepper flakes
The wedding invitation (including the envelope)

Sprinkle the red pepper flakes into the envelope with the invitation inside. Shake it vigorously while picturing a red-hot light around the betrothed couple, and offer this hex:

May you sweat profusely through your wedding attire, causing all your photos to need pit retouching.

PARTNER WHO BREAKS UP WITH YOU VIA TEXT

All relationships, even short or rocky ones, deserve a respectful breakup. However, a few people seem to have skipped this lesson at love school. Some breakups involve screaming, drama, passion, breakup sex. Some are more of a quiet fizzle. But do you know what is never, ever OK? The text breakup. If you're over the age of twelve, you deserve more than a few acronyms and an emoji to mark the end of an affair.

YOU'LL NEED
A nice piece of chocolate
A piece of paper and a pen

Take a moment to sit and enjoy the chocolate. As you savor the flavor, think about what type of kind, gentle breakup letter you should've received—and, on the paper, write it yourself. Mention at least one good thing that you will miss about your relationship, and one bad thing you won't miss. When you're done, tear the paper into tiny pieces and bury it deep in the trash while offering up this hex:

May the next person you're super into
be super into your best friend.

FORMER LOVE WHO
TRASH-TALKS YOU

Really, the nerve! We're not in high school anymore, so unsavory rumor spreading ought to be firmly in the rearview mirror. No grown-ass woman should be worried about her reputation being dragged down by an oversharing ex! Yet you've heard from several sources that a former flame has been dropping your name around town, and not in a nice, respectful way. In a trashy way, like spilling the intimate details of your trysts (with facts wrong to boot). Get some revenge before this gossip spreads further.

YOU'LL NEED

A piece of paper and a pen
Matches or a lighter
A black candle (or any candle placed atop something black)

On one side of the paper, write the name of your former lover. On the other side, write a piece of gossip you've heard. Light the candle, then burn the paper over the candle and say this spell:

You think words don't matter?
Then enjoy this hex.
Because sometime after midnight
You'll drunk-dial your ex.

Essential Empowerment Spell

Still plagued by love trouble that doesn't fit any of the previous scenarios? Fear not. Here's a universal love spell for good fortune in all aspects of romance. It will bolster both your heart and your other essential love organs.

YOU'LL NEED

A piece of paper and a pen
A red candle (or any candle
placed atop something red)
Matches or a lighter

On the paper, draw a heart, then fill it in with your own name, as many times as will fit. Put the paper under the candle. Light the candle and picture your heart glowing a deep, luminous red. Take three deep breaths, then say this spell aloud:

Spirits, protect me from players, haters, and other unworthy partners. May I remember my own unique greatness and allow only those truly deserving of my heart—or body—to come anywhere near it.

Home

Spells

Ah, home sweet home, where everything is calm, soothing, and just how you like it. Except when it isn't! Sometimes home is anything but a sanctuary. It can be the site of a battle of wills with a messy roommate, noisy neighbors, evil landlords, or inconsiderate guests. The good news is, your innate powers are strongest when you are at home, surrounded by your own personal items. So harness that energy and cast these spells to ensure that your home is every bit as sweet as you deserve.

Trouble Inside

OVERPRICED REPAIR PERSON

It's so maddening! There are just certain things you can't fix yourself, and, desperate, you end up at the mercy of someone who claims to be a professional—handyman, plumber, electrician, mechanic. Are they trustworthy? Who knows? The truth is, they know you need them more than they need you. And sometimes they take advantage. If you get a whopper of a bill for a tiny bit of service, don't settle for a negative Yelp review. Give them something extra with this hex:

The next time you need service yourself—whether it's a dental visit, haircut, dog grooming, or something more personal—may you be horrendously overcharged for a terrible job.

RUINER/HOGGER
OF BATHROOM

Wouldn't it be a dream come true to have your very own posh bathroom, all to yourself? Alas, you're stuck in the unfortunate position of sharing with someone terribly messy or ridiculously funky. Until you get your own perfect powder room, though, something can be done. Don't endure a person who repeatedly leaves the bathroom looking or smelling toxic. (And haven't they ever heard of opening a window or lighting a match?) Get back at them with this spell.

YOU'LL NEED

Perfume, lotion, or body spray in your favorite scent
A plunger
A match

Place the delicious-smelling item next to the plunger in your bathroom. Picture the offending person and light the match. As it burns down, say this spell:

You spoil my bathroom;
My anger won't be abated.
But for the next week,
You'll be constipated.

MESSY ROOMMATE

Oh, the joys of sharing your household! Whether your roomie is a friend, a lover, or just someone who's sharing your rent, there's no easy solution when your roommate is simply messier than you. Likely you've tried gentle nudging or even a heart-to-heart already. If you regularly come home to dirty dishes, wet towels on the floor, or an overflowing garbage can, you've got to take things to the next level. Clean house in a whole different way with this powerful hex.

YOU'LL NEED

A dry sponge
Something that belongs to your roommate
(a hairbrush works nicely)
A paper bag
A pinch of dried sage

Put the sponge and personal item in the bag, then sprinkle the outside of the bag with the sage (a powerful herb for cleansing—in all senses of the word). Say this spell, being careful not to spill the sage and have to do even more tidying up!

> *For every mess you make in our lair,*
> *You will get one new gray hair* (somewhere).

HOUSEGUEST WHO OVERSTAYS THEIR WELCOME

There's a reason for that old adage about fish and houseguests starting to smell after three days—this person really stinks! It can be awkward to share your house with someone who just doesn't know when it's time to leave. It's even worse if they don't even know how to be a courteous guest: eating you out of house and home, leaving dishes around, using all the hot water, keeping you up late or waking you up early. (Where's your hostess gift, anyway? And why aren't they making *you* dinner?) When you just can't stand another twenty-four hours of shared quarters, give them a gentle kick in the right direction.

YOU'LL NEED
Your house key
A piece of their luggage or toiletries case

Tap your key on their luggage three times, then separate them as far as possible from each other in the room. Visualize your unwelcome guest packing up. Tuck your key away in a safe place, and then say this hex:

For every day you overstay your welcome,
may your in-laws stay with you an
extra week over the holidays.

TERRIBLE PARTY GUEST

Quelle downer—there's a straight-up party pooper at your shindig! Perhaps you tried to do the right thing and invited a neighbor, friend of a friend, or coworker who you weren't sure about. Or perhaps it's someone you actually thought would be a fun addition. But somehow, you've ended up with a guest who is just the worst: boorish, boring, insulting, drinks too much, drinks too little, says the utterly wrong things, or simply casts a pall on what are otherwise fantastic festivities (if you do say so yourself). Teach them some proper party manners by saying this spell:

Your comportment was lacking,
Your conversation was tired,
Now the best things in your fridge
Will all be expired.

ROOMMATE WHO STOLE YOUR OUTFIT

Sharing your life—bills, chores, food, space—with a roommate will never be without its ups and downs. Even if you're good friends, there can be prickly moments where you disagree about divvying up the chores, or you're just weary of one another. One thing you shouldn't have to deal with? Someone pilfering your fiercest ensemble! If your roomie had the gall to swipe your favorite outfit, she deserves to feel your wrath.

YOU'LL NEED
One of her favorite go-to tops
Her most beloved pair of jeans
Two pieces of black cloth

Lay out the top and jeans. Visualize your roomie on the way to an important night out, when she catches herself in a mirror and sees the outfit just doesn't look right. Put one piece of black cloth on each item and say this spell:

You love this cute top
But a stain has appeared!
And now your best jeans
Look weird from the rear.

SUPER-TIDY FRIEND WHO GIVES YOUR HOME THE SIDE-EYE

OK, so you're not Martha Stewart. So what? Your place is cute, comfortable, and reasonably clean. Sure, maybe there's some cat hair, some unfolded laundry, a few wineglasses in the sink. You're only human. But you have that one friend who never fails to make you feel inferior. If they came over and gave your place attitude, including thinly veiled insults ("Wow, how do you even find the remote in here?" "What's that smell, your cat?" "Oh, your place is always so . . . lived in."), give that dictator of domesticity a taste of their own cleaning spray. (Which is probably organic and homemade.)

YOU'LL NEED

A piece of paper and a pen
Your friend's address
Any smelly item (can of cat food, used gym sock,
old cheese you should throw out, etc.)

On the paper, write down your friend's address and then tuck it inside or beside the smelly item. Visualize your friend and their upturned nose. (This should be easy to do, as it happens frequently.) Say the spell on the next page, repeating it as many times as the number of days you'd like the smell to linger in your judgy friend's abode.

*W*hen you get home
To your picture–perfect place,
There will be a strange smell
You cannot erase!

Trouble Outside

MANHANDLING MOVER

How difficult is it to move a few pieces of furniture from point A to point B with some modicum of care? Apparently very. As if it isn't stressful enough to move, it adds insult to injury if you can't rely on the people who are supposed to make it all go smoothly. If you—and your belongings—have been left feeling dinged, mishandled, and squashed, take a seat on one of those moving boxes and offer up this hex for the jerkwad in charge:

Next time you move, may none of your friends show up—even the one who swore you could borrow their truck.

ANNOYING DOOR-TO-DOOR SALESPERSON

Sure, sometimes people canvass the neighborhood for a good cause. (Hello, Girl Scouts!) But most of the time, when your doorbell rings unexpectedly, it's someone smarmy who's hard-selling something you don't want. And always at inconvenient times. Odds are they're neither courteous, professional, polite, nor quick. If you can't stop the people pushing everything from magazine subscriptions to condos, don't delay: act now for proper payback.

YOU'LL NEED
A sprig of sage (or a pinch of dried sage)

As soon as you shut the door on them, rub a little bit of the sage on the doorknob on both sides of the door to ward off future unwanted guests. Then place both of your hands firmly on your closed, locked front door while visualizing the perpetrator and saying this hex:

Tonight, may your cell-phone number appear on the frequent-call list of every major telemarketing company in Asia.

LANDLORD FROM HELL

All you expect from a landlord is that they keep your place in good working order, and that they are reasonable and prompt when you let them know something is amiss. Why is that so difficult? If you've ever rented, you know that there is almost always something wrong with the landlord. Whether they've been especially greedy, lazy, elusive, or unfair, give them their comeuppance with this spell. (Bonus: This also works for real-estate agents/mortgage brokers from hell.)

YOU'LL NEED

A copy of your lease or other paperwork
that includes your landlord's name
An envelope
A black pen

Put the lease in the envelope and write your landlord's name backward on the outside. Then fold it into thirds away from you while picturing household horrors and saying this curse:

May your rental income dwindle
And also your dreams
As your own house starts falling
Apart at the seams.

PACKAGE SWIPER

No! It can't be. The package you've been waiting for, the one that is absolutely essential and time sensitive (or at least something really cute you've been wanting), has gone missing. Seems like some evil person has been stealing deliveries in your neighborhood, and you're the latest victim. Of course, the item is now back-ordered/unavailable/irreplaceable/too late to be of use. What kind of person would do that? No doubt they deserve some well-timed revenge. Stand in the spot where your package *should* be waiting, and offer this curse to the perpetrator:

You've taken something I wanted,
So this spell's not a joke.
By week's end, you will find yourself
Arrested, lonely, and broke.

NOISY NEIGHBORS

What are they *doing* over there? Do you hear mystery noises above you at weird hours, as if they're rearranging furniture or playing hockey at 2 a.m.? Or do cars constantly come and go next door before dawn? Have you resorted to banging a broom on the ceiling like an old lady, or even calling the cops when parties have gone on too long? Don't start thinking you're crazy. It's not you, it's them. When you live in close proximity to others, some common courtesy is required. When you just can't take it anymore, quiet them down with this ritual.

YOU'LL NEED
A clock
A pillow
A drop of lavender essential oil
(or a pinch of dried lavender)

Set the clock to the time your neighbors normally bother you most. Then sprinkle three drops of the essential oil on the pillow, and cover the clock with it. Inhale the relaxing scent while picturing yourself blissfully a-snooze. After three long and relaxing breaths, turn your thoughts to revenge by saying this spell:

*M*ay you get called for jury duty, and may it be a long, boring trial that starts bright and early every day across town.

DRIVEWAY/PARKING-SPOT BLOCKER

There are certain codes we follow in civilized society, and one involves parking. We simply do not block other people's driveways—and we certainly don't park in someone else's designated parking spot! What are we, animals? If you've found a mystery car in your spot, perhaps you first left a note on the windshield, or asked around to figure out whose car it was. If you did, you are more generous than most. If that car is still there—or if they parked there again!—it's time to call the tow truck. While you're waiting for it to arrive, look at the offending vehicle and say this spell:

I tried to be understanding,
I tried to take heart.
But the next time you're running late,
Your car will not start.

CONSTRUCTION CREW THAT MAKES A PREDAWN RACKET

You realize there are early risers in this world. Maybe you're even one of them (sometimes). And you understand that some jobs must begin in the morning. But dawn is simply too early to be making a racket in a residential neighborhood. Noise ordinances exist for a reason, people! The least the construction crew could do is start with the quieter work, and save the pile driving and jackhammering for a slightly more decent hour, right? But no. It's always the loudest noise and the earliest start for these yahoos. The next time they wake you, get back at them with this spell. (Rest assured, this also works for those who use leaf blowers or lawn mowers before noon on weekends.)

For every day you make a racket too early, may your smoke alarm battery keep chirping in the middle of the night—no matter how often you replace it.

TRASH COLLECTOR WHO KNOCKS OVER YOUR BINS

You manage to get your tied trash bags to the dumpster or trash cans without incident. Yet somehow, week after week, the garbage truck trundles through with ungodly racket at an unholy hour, only to leave upturned bins and drifting trash in its wake. You know that with just a little more effort from the trash collector, just a *smidge*, you and all your neighbors would have a much better morning. Yet every week, you are faced with your very own collection-day trashnado, and it's beginning to feel like the sanitation specialist is screwing up on purpose. This perpetrator better clean up their act. Give them a little nudge with this hex:

You will soon be getting new neighbors: a group of rowdy, messy, inconsiderate college students.

Essential Empowerment Spell

If your home is still not feeling like your castle, get ready to reign with a spell that will remind you who wears the crown. (Psst: It's you!)

YOU'LL NEED

A piece of mail with your address
A pen
Matches or a lighter
A yellow candle (or any candle placed atop something yellow)

On the back of the piece of mail, write down the three absolute best things about your current living situation, no matter how big or small. Light the candle and picture your home bathed in a welcoming, warm yellow light. Take three deep breaths, then say this spell aloud:

Spirits, protect me from bad roommates or landlords, unpleasant domestic crises, and terrible neighbors. Remind me that I am the queen of my castle, and that I have the power to create an environment that is warm, healthy, and appealing to me.

Spells

Ah, it's good to be out and about—if only there weren't other people there, too, making a mess of things! Every time you leave the house, you risk road rage, parking headaches, transit snafus, airport annoyances, and more transport trials. It's bad enough when it's just a regular day. But when you are finally going someplace fun (ahoy, vacation!) and find yourself on the receiving end of bad behavior? That's just too much. The world is a crowded, busy place, so we all have to do our best to go with the flow. If someone doesn't? They've earned themselves a one-way ticket to Revenge City.

Driving Debacles

UTTERLY DIRECTIONALLY CHALLENGED DRIVER

Don't you love it when your taxi/shuttle/Uber/Lyft driver asks *you* the best route to take—even if you're new to town? Or when they're so absorbed in Google Maps that you're worried they aren't even glancing at the road? But the capper is when you realize they are taking you not just the long way but the completely *wrong* way. Make sure they don't drive anyone else this crazy by reciting this hex:

Next time you're off duty
Someplace far from home,
May you find yourself in gridlock
2 percent battery left on your phone.

DRIVER WHO CUT YOU OFF

There are always entitled people on the road. You can tell who they are by how they drive: like they own the place. These self-centered road hogs seem to feel they *deserve* to cut in front of you at the last minute. (These are usually the same folks who drive in the carpool lane solo, pass on a double yellow, and flash their lights if you're going two miles an hour slower than they'd like.) Skip the road rage and get your revenge with this spell—once you're safely parked.

YOU'LL NEED
A piece of paper and a pen
The make and model of the offender's car
Your car keys

If you can remember, on the piece of paper, write down the make and model of the car, as well as where the incident took place. Put your keys on top of the paper and picture the offending car, channeling your anger. After a moment, tear the piece of paper into tiny pieces while saying this spell:

For every person you cut off, may a mysterious and annoying warning light appear on your dash until you have to endure an expensive mechanic visit.

SNOBBY VALET WHO SMIRKS AT YOUR CAR

OK, so your vehicle is not exactly a chariot. It's not new, it's not fancy, and it's maybe not the cleanest car in town. But if you had to pay a fee—and a tip!—to valet park, you expect at least a little decorum. You certainly don't deserve an arched eyebrow from a snooty valet. If you've been the victim of a condescending car jockey, grip your valet stub tightly in your fist and say this spell:

You saw me drive away,
But from me you'll get more.
May your very next customer
Insist you scratched his door.

EVIL PARKING-ENFORCEMENT PERSON

OK, there are situations when a parking ticket is deserved. Like for that human fungus who parked in a handicapped spot "just for a second." But there seem to be certain parking enforcers who take a little too much evil joy in their job, hunting down drivers who made the tiniest infraction—and then not listening to reason. If you only stayed one minute too long at a meter or had a mere inch of your back tire in the yellow, you expect a little bit of a break. But they write you up anyway—and seem happy to hand you that slip of paper that breaks your budget. Drive *them* mad with this spell.

YOU'LL NEED

Matches or a lighter
A photocopy of your parking ticket

You know what to do. Light the copy on fire over the sink while wishing the writer of the ticket a very bad day. Then say this chant:

You make people mad.
You make people panic.
May your car go for service
With a dishonest mechanic.

HANDICAPPED-PARKING-SPOT CHEATER

There's no excuse for it. It doesn't matter if it's raining, or they need to carry something heavy, or if it's "just for a minute." If you parked miles away and witness some entitled jerk hopping nimbly out of their car in a handicapped spot without a handicapped sticker, you need to call them on it. And after you do that, say this hex as a little extra incentive for them to think twice next time:

In the next month, may you be plagued by so many parking and speeding tickets that you have to go to traffic court—on the same day you planned to leave on vacation.

Trouble in Transit

MANSPREADER ON
TRAIN OR BUS

Talk about a space invader! Some people just seem to have no sense of personal space, or if they do, they don't care. They kick their legs open, lean toward you, use both armrests, and generally make you feel like you're snuggling with an unappealing stranger. If you fall victim to someone who has spread all their limbs into your business, cross your own legs and arms tightly, give them a good stare down, and say this hex in your head:

For the next two weeks,
or maybe the next three,
Each time you board a train or a bus,
You'll suddenly have to pee.

COMMUTER WHO PUSHES PAST YOU FOR LAST SPOT

We all might get a little self-centered when we're stressed and in a hurry. From time to time, we might speed walk, cut in front of people on the sidewalk or escalator, or generally forget our best manners. But add in a completely packed train or bus, with clamoring hordes wanting aboard? Then people really become animals. If you were doing the right thing and waiting your turn, only to have an interloper cut in and take your rightful spot, the commuter code has been broken. That queue hopper needs to go down. Fix them with your gaze, and quietly direct this hex at them:

You've made me late and angry,
So revenge is now my job.
You'll jam the door upon leaving,
Earning ire from the angry mob.

CRABBY FLIGHT ATTENDANT

Why do people choose to work in the service industry if they are going to act put out all the time? Sure, a flight attendant's work can be tough. But isn't part of the job description to be kind, friendly, and helpful to customers? These days, when you spend good money on a plane ticket (and extra money if you want legroom, a checked bag, or sustenance during the flight), it would be nice to get a warm welcome from the staff. Instead, you got nothing but high-altitude attitude. So much for the friendly skies.

YOU'LL NEED
Your boarding pass
A pen
The name of your flight attendant

On the boarding pass, write the attendant's name and then fold it three times away from you while saying this spell:

You're acting quite crabby,
Like you're fully in a snit.
On your next flight, the call button
Will always remain lit.

CAR-RENTAL AGENT WHO GAVE YOU A LEMON

How can it possibly cost so much to rent something called an "economy" car? It's bad enough that you always get price gouged. Then you're nickel and dimed for extras, pressured into buying insurance, and required to drive out of your way ten miles to fill up the gas tank. But if this time you also got a crappy car, in which the stereo, navigation system, AC, sunroof, or other promised features didn't work? And then got no sympathy—or discounts—when you reported it to a clearly disinterested employee? Break out this spell.

YOU'LL NEED
A slip of paper and a pen
The name of your agent
A copy of your rental agreement
A lemon
A bag or a sack

On the paper, write the name of your unhelpful agent. Then put the paper, the rental agreement, and the lemon in the bag. Shake the bag three times and say this incantation:

You not only gave me a lemon,
   You also gave me sass.
Next time you drive somewhere
   important
Your own car will run out of gas.

PERSON WHO HOLDS UP ALREADY ENDLESS SECURITY LINE

Airport security lines are the low point of any trip, but how does it happen that you always end up in the wrong one? At the other checkpoint, people are moving right along, removing their shoes and their neatly bagged toiletries, then gliding through the metal detector with nary a beep. But in front of you? It's the person who clearly hasn't flown since 1996. They've got oversize shampoo in their carry-on and various forms of metal on their person, meaning both the conveyer belt *and* the metal detector are backed up. Worse, they keep asking unnecessary questions! It's a preflight fail. While you're waiting, say this little hex to pass the time:

You made the preboarding process
Even longer and more boring.
May you be seated next to someone
Who falls asleep on you (while snoring).

LUGGAGE HANDLER WHO SQUASHED OR LOST YOUR BAG

Nowadays, it can cost a significant chunk of your travel budget just to check a bag. Shouldn't you be rewarded for *not* being one of those people who try to shove a full-size suitcase and a guitar into the overhead bin? Instead, you paid good money, then waited patiently at the luggage carousel, and your reward was a bag that looked positively trampled. Did the airline put the Hulk in charge of this flight's baggage, or what? Of course, all you can do now is wait even longer to talk to a probably ineffective customer-service agent. Or might there be an alternate route to satisfaction?

YOU'LL NEED
A pinch of dried thyme
Your luggage tag

Sprinkle the thyme on the luggage tag while visualizing the creep who mishandled it, then say this hex:

The next time you take a long-awaited flight,
May your bags be lost, with no help in sight.

SMELLY FELLOW PASSENGER WHO ABUSES SHARED SPACE

The list of public transportation transgressions is long and varied. But there is a special circle of hell reserved for someone who eats fast food, removes their shoes (or shoes and socks!), lets farts fly, or otherwise selfishly offends fellow travelers on a plane, train, or bus. Do they not understand that this is shared air, and not everyone wants to smell their Big Mac or compression socks for the entire journey? Clear the air with this spell:

After each olfactory offense,
You will feel my powers,
Because the journey you take next
Will be delayed at least three hours.

Vacation Blunders

KNOW-IT-ALL WHO GAVE YOU AWFUL TRAVEL TIPS

You love recommendations! Who doesn't want insider tips on hidden hotels, interesting restaurants, and off-the-beaten-track sights to see when going to a new place? So, when your "friend" went on and on about being an expert on your destination, you diligently wrote down their top picks and got ready for some amazing experiences. Instead? You wound up with bad directions, tourist traps, and fleabag hotels. (Fingers crossed you didn't pick up any bedbugs!) Pay them back with this hex:

On your next trip, may you get horribly lost and have to spend all evening trying to connect to Wi-Fi in a Jack in the Box . . . with an out-of-service bathroom.

CONSTANTLY COMPLAINING TRAVEL COMPANION

Usually it's nice to share a journey. Someone to split the costs with, eat with, explore with, and even complain with when things go wrong. But when your companion is the only one complaining? That's a nonstarter. If you've been saddled with a travel mate who refuses to be happy with the food, the accommodation, the sights, or the people, it can really put a damper on the whole holiday. Turn things around with this spell.

YOU'LL NEED
A leaf or flower petal
A ticket stub from your travels

Place the leaf or flower on top of the ticket stub, ideally outside or on a windowsill. Visualize this small item growing and blossoming into something amazing and think of all the future trips you have yet to take. Then offer up this spell:

*I'll travel the world
  And never get tired,
While you'll find your passport
Unexpectedly expired.*

HOTEL STAFF MEMBER WHO GIVES YOU A CRUMMY ROOM

All you wanted was a nice, peaceful hotel room. Is that too much to ask? You booked way ahead. You double-checked your reservation. You were extra nice to the person at the front desk when you checked in. Then you used your key and—wait, is this a room or a broom closet? And not only is it tiny—it's noisy. You are right across from both the elevator and the ice machine, and you swear you can hear someone coughing in the next room. This is not what the place seemed like online. If the hotel staff gives you no help whatsoever, it's time to check out—check out this spell, that is.

YOU'LL NEED

Your room key
Dollar bill (any denomination will do)

Wrap the key in the dollar bill and place it at the threshold of your room. Picture the offending person while saying this curse:

Instead of help,
You just gave me lip.
For the rest of the week,
No one here will tip.

BEACH OR POOLSIDE SHOW-OFFS

All you wanted on vacation was a good book and a view of the water. But when you look out from your lounge chair, what do you see? A couple of hot-body show-offs strutting like peacocks in the world's tiniest swimwear. Back and forth, back and forth, stopping only to take selfies or do a handstand by the water, like it's a freaking Hawaiian Tropic competition. Don't let them disturb your bliss. Calmly put on your shades, close your eyes, and offer up this hex:

Yes, we all see your nice bodies
And your lovely faces,
But tomorrow you'll have a sunburn
in your most delicate places.

OVER-THE-TOP PDA COUPLE

Love is grand! You don't mind seeing a little smooch or an affectionate hug between lovers in public, especially when you're somewhere romantic. That's to be expected, and it can be downright sweet. But society draws a line between sweet and unsavory, and this couple has definitely crossed it. If you're by the pool, at a restaurant, on a train, or trapped on tour with a couple who is making out nonstop in front of everyone, use this incantation to throw some water on the situation:

You've made us all queasy,
So here's your diagnosis:
Tomorrow you'll both be plagued
with chronic halitosis.

JERK WHO STEALS YOUR LOUNGE CHAIR OR BARSTOOL

It's the little things on vacation: a nice lounge chair by the pool; a frosty drink at the bar; a peaceful, relaxing few days with no demands and no one bugging you. But if someone swiped your lounge chair or barstool, or took the last pool towel or your spot in line, they've set themselves up as your vacay nemesis. Use this spell to give a fittingly small but annoying payback to the small but annoying person who wronged you:

You think you're entitled,
But we'll take care of that.
All your towels will be damp
And your beer will taste flat.

MISLEADING AIRBNB HOST

You were promised a spacious, light-filled home with two bedrooms and a terrace. It looked fantastic online. Yet, like a bad internet date, the photos you saw were terribly misleading. The place is dark, cramped, and not all that clean. And they forgot to give you any towels! Or toilet paper! Of course, when this happens, the host will either feign confusion about your complaints or not pick up the phone. They didn't make the bed; now let *them* lie in it. Pull up their erroneous listing, write your honest review, and then give them a little something extra with this hex:

Next time you go on vacation, may you get the worst seat on the plane and the loudest neighbor at the hotel, and may your luggage be the last piece on the carousel.

Essential Empowerment Spell

If you still feel thwarted by the masses who can make traveling unbearable, give yourself some well-deserved protection while you're out and about with this spell.

YOU'LL NEED

A piece of paper and a pen
Your car keys or transit pass
Matches or a lighter
A blue candle (or any candle placed atop something blue)

On the paper, write down your very best outing of recent memory—whether it was a weekend road trip, a great night out, or a full-on vacation. Place the paper atop the keys or transit pass. Then light the candle and picture yourself in that place, surrounded by a soothing, cool blue light. Take three deep breaths, then say this spell aloud:

Spirits, protect me from road rage, travel snafus, and painful journeys of all sorts. Remind me that I have the inner moxie to rise above the unpleasantness of getting somewhere, and to enjoy it to the hilt when I arrive.

SPELL FOR BANISHING ANYTHING NEGATIVE

Hopefully this book has helped you to embrace Bitchcraft and your own inner power, and you now feel ready to move past those pesky people who bring you down. But while a whole array of annoyances is included in this book, more will always arise: something unexpected that requires some revenge. If your current problem doesn't fit into any of the specific situations described in the previous pages, fear not. We will finish our work with a general spell to help you deflect any negative energy. Consider this your catchall, an incantation you can use for any occasion. And remember: your intention, your annoyance, and your righteous anger are the most powerful tools in your Bitchcraft toolbox! Harness those, and nothing can stop you.

YOU'LL NEED

A white candle
A white plate
A pinch each of dried sage, lavender, rosemary, and thyme
Matches or a lighter

Put the candle on the plate and sprinkle the herbs around it. Light the candle and think of yourself bathed in a clean white light, free of all the irritating characters who bug you on a daily basis. Take three deep breaths. Then turn your attention to the particular problem at hand. Visualize the wrong that has been done to you, being as specific as possible. Then picture it fading into the white light until it disappears. Offer the spell below, then blow the candle out, stand tall, and move on.

This won't bring me down;
  There's strength in my spell.
I'll rise up and move past it.
My revenge? Living well.